→ **INTRODUCING**

KEYNES

PETER PUGH & CHRIS GARRATT

Published in the UK in 2009
by Icon Books Ltd.,
Omnibus Business Centre,
39–41 North Road, London N7 9DP
email: info@iconbooks.co.uk
www.introducingbooks.com

Sold in the UK, Europe, South Africa
and Asia by Faber and Faber Ltd.,
Bloomsbury House,
74–77 Great Russell Street,
London WC1B 3DA
or their agents

Distributed in the UK, Europe, South
Africa and Asia by TBS Ltd.,
TBS Distribution Centre,
Colchester Road, Frating Green,
Colchester CO7 7DW

This edition published in Australia
in 2009 by Allen & Unwin Pty. Ltd.,
PO Box 8500, 83 Alexander Street,
Crows Nest, NSW 2065

Previously published in the UK and
Australia in 1993 under the title
Introducing Keynesian Economics

This edition published in the USA
in 2009 by Totem Books
Inquiries to: Icon Books Ltd.,
Omnibus Business Centre,
39–41 North Road,
London N7 9DP, UK

Distributed to the trade in the USA by
National Book Network Inc.,
4501 Forbes Boulevard, Suite 200,
Lanham, Maryland 20706

Distributed in Canada by
Penguin Books Canada,
90 Eglinton Avenue East, Suite 700,
Toronto, Ontario M4P 2Y3

ISBN: 978-184831-065-0

Printed by Gutenberg Press, Malta

Keynes is back!

This is what Maynard Keynes (1883–1946) said on the BBC in January 1931 as the whole world, the UK included, slid ever further into the greatest depression of modern times:

> The best guess I can make is that whenever you save five shillings [25p, but about £12 in today's money] you put a man out of work for a day. Your saving that five shillings adds to unemployment to the extent of one man for one day and so on in proportion. On the other hand, whenever you buy goods you increase employment – though they must be British, home-produced goods if you are to increase employment in this country ... Therefore, oh patriotic housewives of Britain, sally out tomorrow early into the streets and go to the wonderful sales that are everywhere advertised. You will do yourself good – for never were things so cheap, cheap beyond your dreams. Lay in stock of household linen, sheets and blankets to supply all your needs. And have the added joy that you are increasing employment, adding to the wealth of our country, because you are setting on foot useful activities, bringing a chance and hope to Lancashire, Yorkshire and Belfast.

This is exactly what the British government (and governments round the world) are trying to persuade their voters, and encouraging them with tax breaks, to do in 2009.

We are all Keynesians now

As Martin Wolf wrote in the *Financial Times* at the end of 2008:

> We are all Keynesians now. When Barack Obama takes office he will propose a gigantic fiscal stimulus package. Such packages are being offered by many other governments. Even Germany is being dragged, kicking and screaming, into this race.

And the long-living Marxist Eric Hobsbawm wrote:

> It is certainly the greatest crisis of capitalism since the 1930s. As Marx and Schumpeter foresaw, globalisation not only destroys heritage, but is incredibly unstable. It operates through a series of crises. There'll be a much greater role for the state one way or another. We've already got the state as lender of last resort, we might well return to the state as employer of last resort, which is what it was under FDR.

As we shall see in this book, Keynes's approach to solving the economic problems of the 1930s – i.e. plunging demand leading to mass unemployment – was adopted in most of the countries of the world and was followed in various ways from the 1930s to the 1970s. However, Prime Minister Margaret Thatcher and President Ronald Reagan, along with their advisers, believed that Keynesianism led to inflation, and as a result it fell out of fashion in the 1980s and 1990s.

Now that we are once again faced with similar economic problems to those of the early 1930s, Keynesianism is once again in favour.

John Maynard Keynes (1883-1946)

John Maynard Keynes was the greatest and certainly the most influential economist of the 20th century. Keynes' economic theories sprang from direct practical experience of three key moments of the 20th century: **the post-World War One peace settlement, the Great Depression** and **World War Two.**

The Keynes Family Background

John Maynard Keynes was born on 5 June 1883 at 6, Harvey Road, Cambridge, a house built by his parents and occupied by them from 1882 until after Maynard's death. His mother, Florence, born in1861, lived there with the same solid furnishings and William Morris wallpaper till she died in 1958.

Keynes' father, **John Neville Keynes (1852-1949)**, had switched from mathematics to moral sciences as a Cambridge undergraduate and became a fellow of Pembroke College after being declared a Senior Moralist, i.e. he came first in the moral science tripos.

Neville was an assistant to the economists Alfred Marshall (1842-1924), who regarded him as one of his best students, and Henry Sidgwick (1838-1900).

Maynard said of his father at a lunch to celebrate his 90th birthday in King's College in 1942:

Neville published two books, *Studies and Exercises in Formal Logic* and *The Scope and Method of Political Economy*. Wittgenstein's biographer, B.F. McGuinness, said of the first book, "still one of the best and most technical expositions of syllogistic logic."

STUDIES AND EXERCISES IN FORMAL LOGIC
by
JOHN NEVILLE KEYNES

THE SCOPE AND METHOD OF POLITICAL ECONOMY
by
JOHN NEVILLE KEYNES

Thereafter, Neville became more involved in administration, symbolized by his election to the University's Council of the Senate in 1892. He became more and more indifferent to strenuous intellectual activity and withdrew into the bosom of his family.

Maynard had been followed by **Margaret**, born 4 February 1885, and **Geoffrey**, born 25 March 1887.

SMILE PLEASE...

Maynard's mother, **Florence Ada Keynes (1861-1958)**, moved into the world of voluntary work and social services. She joined the Cambridge Association for the Care of Girls, the National Association for Physical Education and Improvement and the local Charity Organisation Society.

Keynes' Childhood

Maynard grew up in this solid middle-class intellectual environment and was soon showing signs of precociousness.

He went on to Eton as 10th King's Scholar, mainly on the strength of his mathematics.

Keynes was very successful at Eton where all the scholars lived in the same house, called College, an atmosphere conducive to learning. He was a prodigious prize-winner, gaining 10 in his first year, 18 in his second and 11 in his third, including all the school's main maths prizes.

Significantly for his later success, he had also acquired an excellent command of English. (Maynard's parents had always been great readers, a habit they passed on to their children.)

Maynard was no prig and involved himself, without showing any talent, in several sports.

As Keynes' first biographer, Sir Roy Harrod (1900-78) put it:

Keynes and the Cambridge Apostles

In 1902, Keynes went to King's College, Cambridge, founded in 1441 as a sister foundation of Eton.

HERE WE ARE MR. KEYNES SIR. I'M SURE YOU'LL SOON SETTLE IN.

His Open Scholarship gave him £80 a year with free tuition and rooms. He settled into Cambridge life as easily as Eton's.

Lytton Strachey

Leonard Woolf

WE INVITED HIM TO JOIN THE UNIVERSITY'S MOST EXCLUSIVE SOCIETY...THE CAMBRIDGE CONVERSAZIONE SOCIETY...

...OR APOSTLES, OUR OBJECT IS THE PURSUIT OF TRUTH WITH ABSOLUTE DEVOTION AND UNRESERVE BY A GROUP OF INTIMATE FRIENDS.

The *Apostles,* whose London extension became known as the *Bloomsbury Group,* thought of themselves as "real" and of others as "phenomenal".

Moral Role Model

At this time, Keynes' great ethical hero was **G.E. Moore (1873-1958),** author of *Principia Ethica*. Moore himself had been so religious at school (Dulwich) that from the ages of 13 to 15, when faced with any problem, he would ask:

He then lost his faith and challenged every proposition.

Keynes said of Moore:

"We accepted Moore's religion and discarded his morals. Indeed, in our opinion, one of the greatest advantages of his religion was that it made morals unnecessary - meaning by 'religion' one's attitude to oneself and the ultimate and by 'morals' one's attitude towards the outside world and the intermediate."

Political Role Model

Keynes' great political hero was the Whig writer and philosopher **Edmund Burke (1729-97)**

I ADMIRED HIS CHAMPIONSHIP OF EXPEDIENCY OVER ABSTRACT RIGHT.

Keynes Enters the Civil Service

After Cambridge, Keynes joined the Civil Service and in 1906 became a junior clerk in the military department of the India Office.

I NEVER WENT TO INDIA... AS THE PRINCIPLE STATES; "GOOD GOVERNMENT IS NOT DEPENDENT ON LOCAL KNOWLEDGE, BUT ON APPLYING SOUND UTILITARIAN PRINCIPLES FROM LONDON."

He found little satisfaction in the job.

MY ONE SIGNIFICANT ACHIEVEMENT WAS ARRANGING THE SHIPMENT OF 10 AYRSHIRE BULLS TO BOMBAY!

He returned to Cambridge in 1909, having been elected a prize fellowship at King's on the basis of his thesis on Probability. He moved into a suite of rooms over the gatehouse leading from King's Lane to Webb's Court, which he occupied until his death in 1946.

In October 1911 he became editor of the *Economic Journal* and in 1912 was elected a member of the select Political Economy Club.

The Classical Quantity Theory of Money

Up to 1914, Keynes did not try to develop monetary theory beyond the stage reached by Alfred Marshall, the real founder of English academic economics. Marshall had propounded the view that the very rich and the very poor were the ignoble elements of society.

What does this mean?

Quantity Theorists explained the changes in the **price level** by changes in the supply of money. (Since there was a Gold Standard in those days, this meant that, as all the money was convertible into gold, more money = more gold and vice versa.)
Therefore, by definition, or at least by assumption, the possibility that changes in the **value** of money could affect real demand for goods and services was ruled out.

Was the assumption right?

Wrong, according to Keynes' later ideas. **Right**, according to the belief of the classical economists and the later monetarists.
Yes, the Quantity Theorists' **supply of money** idea is like recent Monetarism. That's why the Monetarists in the 1970s were called "The New Classical Economists", as we shall see later.

21

Thrift was important in classical theory. Otherwise there would be insufficient savings for investment and not enough would be produced to satisfy demand. Both rising and falling prices were unjust. The former penalised savers to the benefit of debtors and the latter brought depression and losses to entrepreneurs.

This simple approach suited Keynes up to 1914. There were no pressing demands in Europe for an improvement on the theory.

The Bloomsbury Group

Keynes graduated from the *Apostles* to the *Bloomsbury Group*, which drew its name from 2 squares in what was the an unfashionable London area. The group was started in 1905 by the four children of **Leslie Stephen (1832-190**

I DUNNO... YOUNG PEOPL TODAY...

POLITICS AND MIDDLE-CLASS SEXUAL CONVENTIONS WERE BANNED AS CANT AND RELIGION WAS DISMISSED.

HOMOSEXUALITY, BISEXUALITY AND PROMISCUITY WERE THE NORM

IT BEGAN WITH OUR THURSDAY EVENINGS.

WE STOOD FOR HONESTY IN CONVERSATION AND PERSONAL RELATIONSHIPS...

...AND A PASSION FOR LITERATURE AND THE VISUAL ARTS.

Virginia

Adrian

Thoby

Vanessa

Keynes

Pioneers of Youth Culture

Leonard Woolf (1880-1969), one of its leading lights, encapsulated Bloomsbury's attitude exactly:

WE WERE CONVINCED THAT EVERYONE OVER 25, WITH PERHAPS ONE OR TWO REMARKABLE EXCEPTIONS, WAS 'HOPELESS,' HAVING LOST THE ELAN OF YOUTH, THE CAPACITY TO FEEL AND THE ABILITY TO DISTINGUISH TRUTH FROM FALSEHOOD...

...WE FOUND OURSELVES LIVING IN THE SPRINGTIME OF CONSCIOUS REVOLT AGAINST THE SOCIAL, POLITICAL, RELIGIOUS, MORAL, INTELLECTUAL AND ARTISTIC INSTITUTIONS, BELIEFS AND STANDARDS OF OUR FATHERS AND GRANDFATHERS...

...WE WERE OUT TO CONSTRUCT SOME--THING NEW; WE WERE IN THE VAN OF THE BUILDERS OF A NEW SOCIETY WHICH SHOULD BE FREE, RATIONAL, CIVILIZED, PURSUING TRUTH AND BEAUTY. Ω

NEVER TRUST ANYONE OVER 25 30 35 40

BORN

The word *Bloomsbury* was to pass into the English language as a cultural phenomenon rather than a geographical area. Keynes entered this way of life with enthusiasm and supported some of the poorer members financially. His great love affair of the time was with the artist **Duncan Grant (1885-1978)**, a cousin of **Lytton Strachey (1880-1932)**.

I WAS IN LOVE WITH GRANT TOO, BUT ALAS, MY LOVE WENT UNREQUITED.

Keynes, always keen on statistics, whether on the economy, cricket or golf, kept full details of his sexual encounters both with Grant and others, entering them in his diary. At a time when any homosexual act was a criminal offence, Keynes identified them with initials, nicknames or simply descriptions.

4 Tuesday
Bank Holiday (Scotland only)

B.G. 3.30pm.

5 Wednesday

Cookie.

17 Sunday
Last Sunday after Pentecost

Auburn-haired of Marble Arch

10 Friday
Ember Day

Stable Boy. Park Lane!!

11 Saturday
Ember Day

Jew Boy.

Thursday **30**

lift boy of Vauxhall. 8.00.

Friday **31**

27

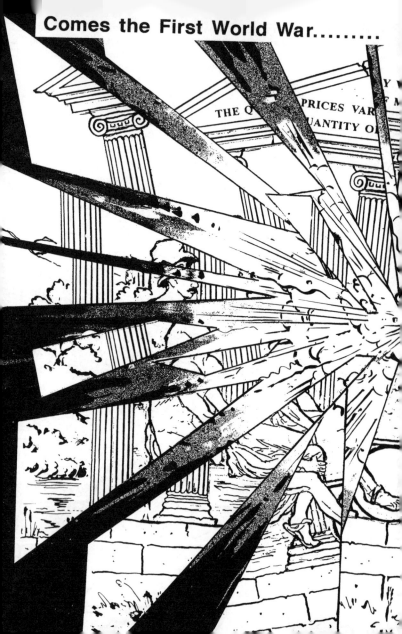

With the outbreak of War in 1914, Keynes moved into the Treasury and was soon advising at the highest level. It could be argued that he was instrumental in bringing the Americans into the War...

...BY PERSUADING THE BRITISH GOVERNMENT TO MAINTAIN CONVERTIBILITY IN EARLY 1917...

...AND THAT'S GOOD FOR US, SINCE WE'VE GOT MOST OF THE WORLD'S GOLD!

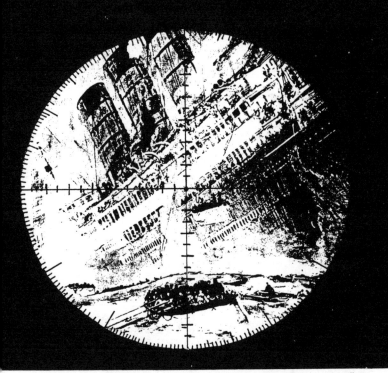

The Germans increased their submarine activity, a key factor in persuading the Americans to declare War. Keynes was promoted to head a new department to deal with all the questions of external finance.

VERSAILLES TREATY SIGNED!

In 1919, at the Paris Peace Conference in Versailles, Keynes was in charge of financial matters and for two months had been preparing the Treasury position on the level of German indemnity payments.

IN OTHER WORDS, REPARATION PAYMENTS!

THE PEOPLES OF BRITAIN AND FRANCE, EGGED ON BY THEIR GOVERNMENTS...

...ARE CLAMOURING FOR GERMANY TO PAY THE FULL COST OF ITS AGGRESSION.

Wilson
USA

Clemenceau
France

Lloyd George
Britain

GERMANY TO PAY £24 BILLION REPARATIONS!

The War Cabinet appointed a committee, largely under the influence of the Bank of England, which recommended a figure of **£24 billion** (£1000 billion in today's terms).

THAT'S RIDICULOUS! DAMN NINCOMPOOP BANKERS!

Keynes' team produced two figures -

COST OF AGGRESSION £4 BILLION

GERMANY'S CAPACITY TO PAY £3 BILLION

IN FACT THE ALLIES WILL BE LUCKY TO GET **2** BILLION!

The Allies,
who had lent money
to many European countries
but had borrowed from the USA,
were worried that they might be left with
bad debts in Europe and firm commitments to the US.
Keynes devised "a grand scheme for the rehabilitation of
Europe", which entailed a scaling down of Britain's demands
on Germany, in return for a remission of some of its debt to the US.

All inter-Ally debts would be reduced and European credit would be revised. The US would be assured of demand for its exports and the Central Powers - the former enemy - would obtain funds to feed their people.

U.S. SAYS: THANKS - BUT NO THANKS!

The U.S. did not buy Keynes' proposition.

Keynes resigned his position at the Treasury to write *The Economic Consequences of the Peace*, one of the most important and influential books of the 20th century.

The Economic Consequences of the Peace

In it, Keynes attacked the three main leaders of the Allies

The Remarkable Foresight of J.M. Keynes

He wrote:
"I am utterly worn out mentally and nervously and deeply disgusted, depressed and dismayed at the unjust and unwise proposals we have made to Germany."

How did Keynes measure Germany's capacity to pay reparations?

"Her only means of paying was through an export surplus. Pre-War her deficit had been £74 million. By reducing imports and increasing exports, she might turn this into a £50 million surplus. Spread over 30 years this would come to a capital sum of £1700 million invested at 6%. Add £100-200 million for transfers of gold, property etc. and £2 billion is a safe maximum figure of Germany's capacity to pay."

"I do not believe that any of these tributes will continue to be paid, at the best, for more than a very few years. They do not square with human nature or agree with the spirit of the age."

He put forward the alternative.

GERMAN DAMAGES LIMITED TO £2000 MILLION

CANCEL INTER-ALLY DEBTS

CREATION OF EUROPEAN FREE TRADE AREA.

International Loan to Stabilize Exchanges.

Encouragement of Germany's natural organizing role in Eastern Europe, including Russia.

And if Keynes' measures were not adopted, what then?

"Vengeance, I dare predict, will not be limp. Nothing can delay for long that final civil war between the forces of reaction and the despairing convulsions of revolution, before which the horrors of the late German war will fade into nothing and will destroy, whoever is the victor, the civilization and progress of our generation."

John Maynard Keynes.

Keynes' book became world-famous, bringing praise from all sides.

Arthur Pigou (1877-1959), who succeeded Marshall as Professor of Political Economy at Cambridge, spoke for the economic establishment.

Others have since argued that its influence damaged world affairs, for 3 reasons:

43

For Keynes' biographer, **Robert Skidelsky (b.1939)**,

IT MARKED A RADICAL SHIFT IN KEYNES' THOUGHT FROM THE 19TH CENTURY ASSUMPTION OF AUTOMATIC ECONOMIC PROGRESS SUSTAINED BY LIBERAL INSTITUTIONS TO A VIEW OF THE FUTURE IN WHICH PROSPERITY WOULD HAVE TO BE STRENUOUSLY WON IN THE TEETH OF THE ADVERSE CIRCUMSTANCES WHICH THE WAR HAD CREATED.

After the War, Keynes returned to Cambridge where he taught, lectured and wrote. From 1922, he lectured on the *Theory of Money* before changing, in 1932, to the *Monetary Theory of Production*. He continued his association with Bloomsbury which remained a strong influence culturally, if not in any other sense.

BLOOMSBURY WAS THE CONDUIT FOR SUCH INTELLECTUAL GIANTS AS DOSTOEVSKY, PROUST, CHEKHOV, CEZANNE, MATISSE, PICASSO AND FREUD.

Keynes supplemented his income through journalism, writing for *The Sunday Times*, the *Manchester Guardian*, the *Evening Standard* and *The Nation* (later absorbed by the *New Statesman*), and the American magazines *Everybody's* and *New Republic*.

THE TIMES — WEATHERCOCK OF THE BRITISH ESTABLISHMENT — REMAINED HOSTILE FOLLOWING MY CRITICISMS OF THE VERSAILLES 'PEACEMAKERS'.

He also indulged in currency speculation. Although nearly cleaned out in 1920, he bounced back to make steady profits throughout the decade.

THUD!

Keynes Marries a Russian Ballerina

He abandoned his homosexual affairs when he met and fell in love with the Russian dancer, **Lydia Lopokova (1892-1981).** They were married in 1925. It had *not* been love at first sight......

But when they met, Keynes was overcome by her charm. There were no children from their marriage, but Lydia was a great source of joy to Keynes for the rest of his life.

Having received little formal education, Lydia was nevertheless a highly intelligent, free spirit. Her English could be idiosyncratic, described by Keynes as *"Lydiaspeak"*.

I HAD TEA WITH LADY GREY. SHE HAS AN OVARY WHICH SHE LIKES TO SHOW EVERYONE.

NOW YOU BOYS WILL WANT TO DO YOUR LITTLE WATERS IN HERE....

47

Lydia was not accepted by all of Keynes' friends. Leonard and Virginia Woolf were highly critical of her, as indeed they were of Keynes, who, they thought, had a brilliant mind but a poor character.

48

It was probably for Lydia that Keynes provided the funds to build the Cambridge Arts Theatre in the 1930s.

The need for a theatre was pressing because the town's two commercial theatres had closed. The New Theatre had become a cinema and the Festival Theatre, which had enjoyed a reputation beyond Cambridge in the late 1920s and early 1930s, had run out of wealthy backers. Furthermore, the ADC suffered a fire and lost its stage in November 1933.

The new Arts Theatre, financed by Keynes, opened on February 3rd 1936, the eve of publication of the *General Theory*, with a programme featuring the Vic-Wells Ballet.

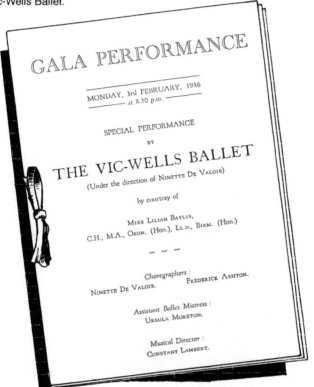

GALA PERFORMANCE

MONDAY, 3rd FEBRUARY, 1936
at 8.30 p.m.

SPECIAL PERFORMANCE

BY

THE VIC-WELLS BALLET
(Under the direction of NINETTE DE VALOIS)

by courtesy of

MISS LILIAN BAYLIS,
C.H., M.A., OXON. (Hon.), LL.D., BIRM. (Hon.)

... ...

Choreographers :
NINETTE DE VALOIS.   FREDERICK ASHTON.

Assistant Ballet Mistress :
URSULA MORETON.

Musical Director :
CONSTANT LAMBERT.

It continued with a season of 4 Ibsen plays, in the first and last of which Lydia took the female leads. In 1938, Keynes transformed the theatre into a trust and it has continued to operate successfully ever since.

Return to the Gold Standard

Keynes spent much of the 1920s arguing against Britain's return to the Gold Standard at sterling's pre-War dollar parity of $4.86. In 1923 he published *A Tract on Monetary Reform*, arguing that Britain should not go back to the pre-War Gold Standard system.

THE GOVERNMENT HAS EVERY INTENTION OF SO DOING!

WELL AT LEAST IT SHOULDN'T BE AT THE PRE-WAR PARITY.

THIS IS YOUR BEST BOOK, MAYNARD!

Milton Friedman

Its central theme is that monetary policy should be used to stabilize the price level and also the demand for money. By varying the amount of credit available to business, the fluctuations in the business cycle could be ironed out.

A Preview of the Exchange Rate Mechanism?

INFLATION IS UNJUST AND DEFLATION INEXPEDIENT. OF THE TWO, PERHAPS DEFLATION IS THE WORSE.

IT IS WORSE, IN AN IMPOVERISHED WORLD, TO PROVOKE UNEMPLOYMENT THAN TO DISAPPOINT THE RENTIER.

In Keynes' view, the management of domestic prices in the interests of business and social stability would be impossible if Britain returned to the Gold Standard at the pre-War parity. Faced with a choice, price stability was more important than **exchange rate stability.**

SOUNDS LIKE THE EUROPEAN COMMUNITY'S EXCHANGE RATE MECHANISM THAT WE ABANDONED IN 1992!

John Major

I WONDER WHAT KEYNES WOULD HAVE THOUGHT OF THE E.R.M.?

Norman Lamont

I GIVE YOU ONE GUESS!

JMK

THE CONTRACTS AND BUSINESS EXPECTATIONS WHICH ASSUME A STABLE EXCHANGE MUST BE FAR FEWER, EVEN IN A TRADING COUNTRY SUCH AS ENGLAND, THAN THOSE WHICH PRESUME A STABLE LEVEL OF INTERNAL PRICES.

Exchange rate policy should be subordinated to the needs of the domestic economy. As most of the world's gold was in the US, a return to the Gold Standard would sacrifice the economic control to the federal Reserve Board of the US.

THE U.S. FEDERAL RESERVE BOARD IN THOSE DAYS ... AND TODAY THE GERMAN BUNDESBANK?

Britain's economy on fast track to recovery in 1992.

Contrary to the classical view, Keynes felt that economic health was too important to be left to a **laissez-faire** approach - or to 'market forces'.

ECONOMIC MANAGEMENT MUST BE PART OF GOVERNMENT!

OH?

As for financial journalists, Keynes wrote to *The Times* on March 28th 1925:

> To debate monetary reform with a City editor is like debating Darwinism with a bishop 60 years ago. But even bishops - so why not City editors? - move in the end.
>
> Yours Faithfully,
> JOHN MAYNARD KEYNES,
> Kings College,
> Cambridge.

He wrote to Lydia:

No! The economist is not king; quite true. But he ought to be. He is a better and wiser governor than the general or the diplomatist or the oratorical lawyer. In the modern, over-populated world, which can only live at all by nice adjustments, he is not only useful but necessary.

Must stop now and catch the post.

love Maynard X.

Keynes lost and in 1925, with Winston Churchill as Chancellor of the Exchequer, Britain returned to the Gold Standard with the pound fixed at its pre-War parity of $4.86. This prompted Keynes to write *The Economic Consequences of Mr.Churchill.*

The policy of improving the exchange by 10% involves a reduction of 10% in the sterling receipts of our export industries. The policy of reducing credit would only reduce wages and the cost of living by creating unemployment. Deflation does not reduce wages automatically. **It reduces them by causing unemployment**.

55

Whatever the argument for a return to the Gold Standard, mainly that the 19th century had been a long period of economic stabiltiy and steady growth, history is on Keynes' side. Virtually everyone is now agreed that the pound was overvalued between 1925 and 1931.

JUST AS THE POUND WAS OVERVALUED WHEN WE CAME OUT OF THE E.R.M. IN 1992.

When at last Britain came off the Gold Standard in 1931, Keynes wrote:

By the return to the gold standard in 1925, at an unsuitable parity, the bank had set itself a problem of adjustments so difficult as to have been well-nigh impossible. On the one hand <u>it was obviously impractical to enforce,</u> by high bank rate or by the contraction of credit, <u>a deflation sufficiently drastic to bring about a reduction in internal costs</u> appropriate to the parity adopted. On the other hand the maintenance of a low bank rate which would have rendered London unattractive to foreign short-term funds would have led to a rapid loss of gold by the Bank and a much earlier collapse of the Gold Standard.

TAP-TAP-TAP-TAP-TAP-TAP-TAP-TAP-RING

The actual course adopted by the bank was a middle way, and as a result, the insecure structure collapsed.

Some prices, such as those determined internationally, rose rapidly, others less so. Wages adjusted even more slowly. The worst affected were those companies deeply involved in the export trade and a massive trade deficit was only averted by keeping the general economy depressed. Keynes criticised the policy of the Bank of England and its restriction of credit.

Full Steam Ahead - to the Crash!

While Britain struggled with high unemployment throughout the 1920s, the US prospered. Unemployment was very low and production, wages and profits rose steadily, year after year. Prices remained stable and economists and politicians felt that the country was not just experiencing the upswing of the normal trade cycle, because this should have brought rising prices.

THE PRESENT LEVEL OF STOCK PRICES DISCOUNTS NOT JUST THE FUTURE BUT THE HEREAFTER!

on the shares of those companies benefiting from this "permanent" rise in profits. Share prices rose to ridiculous levels.

59

The Wall Street Crash - and World Depression

The Crash came in October 1929, and within a month,

shares had fallen by

a third.

They paused and even rose slightly in April 1930. This was a dead cat bounce; they then plunged again and carried on falling for another 2 years.

By the middle of 1932, the average industrial share was about 15% of its price in October 1929. If the Wall Street Crash ushered in the World Slump of the early 1930s, it wasn't the real cause.

The real cause was the good, old fashioned

Upswing - Downswing of the trade cycle.

The upswing in the 1920s had been really strong.

THE OUTPUT OF CAPITAL GOODS ROSE BY NEARLY A QUARTER BETWEEN 1927 AND 1929...

The downswing, which actually began *before* the Wall Street Crash, was going to be strong too.

...BY 1932, THE OUTPUT OF CAPITAL GOODS WAS ONLY A QUARTER OF THE LEVEL OF 1929...

The fall in the output of consumer goods, though less severe, was also strong, and as a result industrial production in 1932 was only half what it had been in 1929.

...UNEMPLOYMENT IN THE U.S. ROSE FROM 1½ MILLION IN 1929 TO 12 MILLION IN 1932.

The Effect on Germany

The repercussions were felt throughout the world, because of the precarious nature of international debt. The US had invested heavily overseas in the 1920s, especially in Germany. Towards the end of the 1920s, US investment in Germany declined.....

.......German industry, starved of funds, began to contract and Germany could not meet reparation and other debt repayments to France and Britain. This led to the same scramble for cash that had accompanied the Wall Street Crash. The spiral worsened............

The Fall and Rise of
John Maynard Keynes

As in the 1920s' slump, Keynes was again almost wiped out personally.

However, he survived, and by 1936 he had rebuilt his fortune to £500,000 (probably £25 million in 2000 terms).

Most of his gains were made in the US, where Wall Street tripled from its low point in 1932, while London stocks hardly appreciated. This was interesting, in view of the fact that Keynes publicly disagreed with his closest City associate, **Oswald Falk (1881-1972),** following Falk's memorandum in 1930.

MEMORANDUM

Date: April 1930

From: Oswald Falk

To: British investors
    Stockbrokers
    Financial Advisers
    Anyone with a bit of Spare Cash

British Industry is finished.

Investors should sell their British securities and buy U.S. ones.

Yrs, Oswald X.

INVESTORS OUGHT TO SHOW MORE CONFIDENCE IN BRITISH INDUSTRY!

BUT—AREN'T YOU MAKING YOUR FORTUNE ON WALL STREET?

The General Theory, 1936

The world depression provided the background for Keynes' seminal work, *The General Theory of Employment, Interest and Money,* published in 1936. If *The Economic Consequences of the Peace* was one of the most influential books of the 20th century, *The General Theory* is probably <u>the</u> most influential.

Paul Samuelson (b.1915), economist and Keynes disciple

"It is a badly written book, poorly organized...it is arrogant, bad-tempered, polemical........it abounds in mare's nests and confusions: involuntary unemployment, wage units, the equality of savings and investments, the timing of the multiplier, interactions of marginal efficiency upon the rate of interest and many others.......flashes of insight and intuition intersperse tedious algebra. An awkward definition suddenly gives way to unforgettable cadenza. When it is finally mastered, we find its analysis to be obvious and at the same time new. In short, it is a work of genius."

Long before 1936, Keynes was a world-renowned figure, ensuring that anything he wrote would be instantly absorbed by anyone influential in the world of finance and economics throughout the world. On both sides of the Atlantic, it was the young economists who took to the book most fervently.

Keynes - The 'Einstein of Economics'

One of the sharpest critics of *The General Theory* was **Arthur Pigou (1877-1959)**. A pioneer of welfare economics, he had himself produced a general economic theory of government intervention. He saw *The General Theory* as a criticism of Marshall and of his own *Theory of Unemployment* (1933).

"Einstein actually did for Physics what Mr. Keynes believes himself to have done for Economics. Einstein developed a far-reaching generalization under which Newton's result can be subsumed as a special case. But he did not, in announcing his discovery, insinuate, through carefully barbed sentences, that Newton and those who had hitherto followed his lead were a gang of incompetent bunglers."

IF I'M THE "EINSTEIN", WHO WERE THE FORMER "NEWTONS" OF ECONOMICS?

In other words, what did Keynes revolutionize? Let's look at economics before Keynes.

Economics before Keynes

For practical purposes, the founder of modern economics was **Adam Smith (1723-90)**, who published his *Wealth of Nations* in 1776. There was no discussion of unemployment.

Smith was followed by **David Ricardo, (1772 - 1823)**, a wealthy stockbroker and MP, who published the first edition of his *Principles of Political Economy and Taxation* in 1817.

EVERYONE WHO WANTS A JOB HAS ONE OR CAN GET ONE.

SMITH'S MAIN CONCERN WAS ECONOMIC GROWTH.

MY MAIN INTEREST IS THE DISTRIBUTION OF THE NATION'S INCOME BETWEEN THE MAIN SOCIAL CLASSES, — LANDOWNERS, CAPITALISTS AND WORKERS...I.E. RENT, PROFIT AND WAGES.

Ricardo's Reply

It is possible to have a glut of commodities, but only a **temporary** glut of a **particular** commodity. Some sudden shock - a war, a change in taxation or of fashion - can bring a decline in demand and consequent unemployment for those producing the commodity. However, as demand for one commodity falls, demand for another will rise. Before long, equilibrium will have been re-established. The only unemployment, of men or machinery, that is possible is temporary unemployment.

Ricardo's reply to Malthus became the enduring thesis of orthodox economists from the 1820s to the 1920s.

RICARDO CONQUERED ENGLAND AS COMPLETELY AS THE HOLY INQUISITION CONQUERED SPAIN!

RIGHT!

Say's Law

To refute Malthus' view of the spectre of general unemployment, Ricardo invoked Say's Law. **J.B. Say (1776-1832)** was a French economist who in 1803 put forward the view that "supply creates its own demand."

IN OTHER WORDS, THE PROCESS OF PUTTING A COMMODITY ON THE MARKET **CREATES** THE INCOME WITH WHICH THAT COMMODITY CAN BE BOUGHT.

Exactly enough income is generated to enable a population to buy everything that is produced.

BY DEFINITION, A GLUT OF COMMODITIES IS IMPOSSIBLE.

BUT... SUPPOSE CAPITALISTS **SAVE** SOME OF THEIR PROFITS. SURELY THEN THERE WOULD BE A GLUT?

NO. THE SAVING IS INVESTED, NOT IN CONSUMER GOODS BUT IN MACHINERY AND BUILDINGS.

MALTH & RICA

AT THE TIME, RICARDO WAS RIGHT. BUSINESSMEN DID INVEST THEIR PROFITS.

They had to, since there was no Stock Exchange for the raising of capital and bank lending was undeveloped.

73

Marx on the Trade Cycle

After Ricardo came **Karl Marx (1818-83)** who took over much of Smith and Ricardo's thinking, but asked a different question.

BOOM

BUST

WHY IS THERE SO MUCH PERIODIC UNEMPLOYMENT?

HE SAW IT AS THE CONSEQUENCE OF THE TRADE CYCLE.

In Marx's view, the trade cycle of boom and bust would get larger and larger, until the whole capitalist system collapsed.

He also saw the economies being increasingly dominated by large monopolies which would invest only **part** of their profits.

Was Marx Right?

With the mass unemployment of the 1920s, Marx's predictions seemed to have come true. The revolution that he had predicted had also come about - though, contrary to his expectation, in Russia - and it was to Soviet communism that many of the most intelligent and thoughtful looked for a solution.

WHAT THIS INTELLIGENTSIA OVERLOOKS IS MARX'S FORMULA THAT THE WORKERS' STANDARD OF LIVING WILL REMAIN AT SUBSISTENCE LEVEL.

In reality, even in the slump year of 1930, the British working man was twice as well off as his grandfather in 1860. Nevertheless Marx made a valid point.....

SOCIETY'S CAPACITY TO PRODUCE WILL OUTSTRIP ITS CAPACITY TO CONSUME.

The Trade Cycle

The other major development in 19th century economic thinking was the acceptance of the **trade** or **business cycle.** The cycle was believed to last 8 to 10 years.

After 3 or 4 more years of decline, everything levels off and begins to rise, setting the whole cycle in motion again.

By the early years of the 20th century, a great deal of thought had been given to the trade cycle throughout the industrialized world and a consensus had been reached on what **caused** the turns in the cycle.

A Difference between Capital Goods and Consumer Goods

What caused the downturn was that industries making **capital** goods, i.e. machinery and equipment used in the processes of production, expanded faster than those making **consumer** goods, i.e. goods bought in shops. As a result, when full employment was reached, production was distorted, with too much labour and money tied up in the production of capital as opposed to consumer goods.

The Accelerator

Why did the upswing bring a greater expansion of capital goods industries? The answer was **The Accelerator.** A small change in the demand for consumer goods leads to a **greater** change in the demand for the capital goods required to <u>produce</u> those consumer goods.

Example

A firm produces 10,000 electric toasters and sells them at £10 each. This production requires £400,000 of machinery.

Each year, 10% of its plant becomes obsolete, so it must buy £40,000 of new plant.

This could continue in equilibrium for ever but in an upswing, the demand for its toasters might increase, say 10%, to 11,000 toasters.

It already takes £40 of machinery to produce each toaster (£400,000 divided by 10,000) and the firm must now install another £40,000 of plant to make the extra toasters.

In that year it must increase its investment from £40,000 to £80,000, an increase of **100%**, to cope with an increase in consumer demand of **10%.**

Recession

And of course the same **Accelerator Principle** applies in reverse. When consumer demand drops back, the capital goods manufacturers' need to buy new plant drops back, again by a much bigger percentage.

IN THE 1920s WE THOUGHT SOMETHING MUST HAVE INTERRUPTED THE NATURAL COURSE OF EVENTS.

—AND THAT 'SOMETHING' IS WAGES NOT FALLING ENOUGH!

KETTLE

HEATING STAND

TOAST RACK

Between 1913 and 1920, wages had risen very sharply. In fact, they had trebled.

SO THEY THOUGHT FULL EMPLOYMENT COULD ONLY BE RESTORED IF WAGES FELL.

The severe recession which began in 1920 did bring, as theory and experience suggested, a sharp fall in both wages and prices, and both declined by about a third in the next three years. However, British exports were still not competitive at the pre-War parity of $4.86 that the government used to take Britain back on to the Gold Standard.

WAGES WILL HAVE TO FALL STILL FURTHER AND WE BELIEVE THEY'LL DO SO AUTOMATICALLY.

I DOUBT THEY WILL WITHOUT FURTHER SAVAGE DEFLATIONARY MEASURES!

With unemployment already over 10%, Keynes felt this was too high a price for returning to the Gold Standard.

The General Strike of 1926

Mine-owners especially disagreed with Keynes and, pressured by the overvaluation of sterling's effect on their export prices, attempted to reduce wages by 10-25%. This led to the **General Strike** in 1926.

But in most other industries, wages stayed at 1925 levels and British exports remained uncompetitive for the rest of the decade. Unemployment also remained high.

Winston Churchill defended the return to the Gold Standard.

Orthodox 1920s economists said...

By 1931, especially in view of the sharp deterioration in the world situation, something had to give. By the end of July, the Bank was losing gold at the rate of £15 million a week and Britain's reserves were down to £133 million.

A Committee on National Expenditure was set up under **Sir George May (1871-1946)**.

WE RECOMMEND INCREASES IN TAXATION AND *DRASTIC CUTS* IN EXPENDITURE, PARTICULARLY ON UNEMPLOYMENT BENEFITS.

THIS IS THE MOST FOOLISH DOCUMENT I HAVE EVER HAD THE MISFORTUNE TO READ!

COMMITTEE ON NATIONAL

This report spread alarm further and the outflow of gold increased. Eventually, with the remaining reserves of gold disappearing, the government suspended gold payments.

The immediate effect was a plunge in the value of sterling from $4.86 to $3.58, a devaluation of 26%. This initially made British exports more competitive but other countries also devalued, raising tariffs in a vain attempt to protect employment. The effect on world trade was catastrophic. It fell to a third of its 1929 level. Unemployment in Britain reached 22%. In Germany and the U.S. it was even higher.

In the 1990s, we again faced the twin evils of recession and unemployment ... and there is still the threat of a trade war.

What's the answer?

The orthodox response from those steeped in 19th century economic thinking was that full employment was the normal state of affairs and, given time, would return.

89

Keynes' Solutions

So much for the orthodox view. In **The General Theory**, Keynes proposed something new and different. In January 1935, he wrote to **George Bernard Shaw (1856-1950)**:

...I believe myself to be writing a book on economic theory which will largely rationalise (not, I suppose at once but in the course of the next few years) the way the world thinks about economic problems....

Keynes rejected the classical Benthamite belief in the **laissez-faire** free market and minimal state intervention.

Jeremy Bentham
1748-1832

...WHERE INDIVIDUAL SELF-INTEREST DOES NOT PRODUCE THE IDEAL, I WANT THE STATE TO INTERVENE, SETTING BOUNDARIES AND DETERMINING RULES FOR DEATH DUTIES, INCOME, REDISTRIBUTION AND THE REGULATION OF MONEY.

He realized that the classical remedies - "to do nothing and wait for full employment to return automatically" - would no longer suffice.

Times had changed from when the high savings of the wealthy in the 19th century had brought a high rate of investment, sustaining progress and raising living standards.

He was conscious of the importance of business confidence.

Is the answer full employment?

Keynes challenged the accepted doctrine that the norm was full employment. "Why should it be?", he asked. This startled the orthodox, but it also carried a strong implication - that if full employment was not automatic, governments were **obliged** to act to bring it about.

What determines the level of employment?

For Keynes, the **level of output** determines the **level of employment.**
This in turn is determined by the level of effective demand, or the level of purchases of goods and services.

THE PURCHASES WILL EITHER BE CONSUMPTION OR INVESTMENT. IF THESE ARE NOT SUFFICIENT TO ABSORB THE COUNTRY'S CAPACITY TO PRODUCE, THERE WILL BE UNEMPLOYMENT... ...AND UNEMPLOYMENT WILL CONTINUE TILL THE LEVEL OF PURCHASES INCREASES.

CONTRARY TO WHAT ECONOMISTS HAVE BEEN SAYING BEFORE, THERE ARE NO AUTOMATIC FORCES GUARANTEEING A RETURN TO FULL EMPLOYMENT.

HEAVY UNEMPLOYMENT MAY PERSIST FOR YEARS (IT HAS, AFTER ALL, NOT BEEN LOWER THAN 10% IN BRITAIN SINCE 1920.)

To Keynes it was more sensible to employ people to do something - anything - as long as they were paid, rather than have them stand idle and be paid little or nothing. As usual he expressed his views graphically:

Government action was necessary, perhaps by reducing interest rates or through public investment programmes.

In conjunction with the effect of the **Multiplier**, such actions should bring back full employment.

95

What is the Multiplier?

The **Multiplier** is tied up with the individual's **marginal propensity to consume** (MPC), which is the fraction of an individual's *increase* in income spent on consumption.

Example

increase in income	=	£1000
spending on consumption	=	£ 800

MPC = 800/1000 or 0.8

Marginal propensity to *save* = 200/1000 or 0.2

KETTLE

HEATING STAND

TOAST RACK

The Multiplier Effect...

For Keynes, the size of the **marginal propensity to consume** (MPC) was the key to the size of the change in the National Income necessary to bring about the ideal equilibrium in which producers would *produce* what consumers wanted to *consume*.

........or the MPC chain......

WHEN I SPEND £800 OF MY £1000 INCREASE...

Mr Heel
the shoemaker

...I RECEIVE HIS £800, BUT I ALSO HAVE AN 0.8 MPC...

Ms Sole
the fishmonger

SO I GET **HIS** 0.8 M.P.C. £640...

Mr Chop
the butcher

...AND I GET **HER** 0.8 M.P.C. £512 ETC. ETC...

97

So........
the final multiplier effect won't be £1000 but

£1000 + £800 + £640 + £512 +........

The final multiplier effect should be a factor of **5**.

Keynes owed a great debt for the development of the Multiplier theory to his "favourite pupil", **Richard Kahn.**

Which countries first tried Keynesian economics?

It is generally accepted that 3 major economies tried Keynesian solutions in the 1930s.
Sweden, Germany and the **US** were influenced by economists moving along the same road as Keynes.

In 1932, **Sweden** returned a Labour government committed to a programme of public investment. Sweden had not suffered in the depression as much as some other countries. Industrial production in 1932 was 89% of its 1929 level, compared with 84% in Britain, 72% in France and 53% in Germany and the US.

.......but unemployment had still increased sharply.

However, recovery was swift. By 1934, real output had regained its 1929 level and by 1935 was 7% above it. Growth continued in the second half of the 1930s and the finance minister was happy to increase the budget deficit to stimulate the economy. He was influenced by a group of economists, particularly Gunnar Myrdal, who had been thinking along Keynesian lines for a number of years.

The German Example

Germany also achieved dramatic growth from its low point of 1932.
In that year, industrial production was more than 40% below its 1929 level and there were 6 million people unemployed. By 1938, industrial production was 25% above the 1929 level and unemployment had been virtually eliminated.

Was Adolf Hitler aware of Keynes?

Keynes certainly did not approve of Hitler's authoritarian methods.

Nevertheless, one of the Nazis' political ambitions - the abolition of mass unemployment - accorded exactly with that of Keynes. Hitler did not have to worry about the Reichsbank whining about balanced budgets.

Final Solution not Keynesian Solutions

On May 1st, 1933, Hitler announced his 4-Year Plan for abolishing unemployment. On the demand side there was the Reinhardt Programme of public works. This was financed, not by borrowing (in 1933, no-one would lend money - even to the government)..

BUT BY ISSUING BILLS WHICH THE REICHSBANK WAS ORDERED TO DISCOUNT!

On the supply side, unemployment was attacked by a whole series of measures, including a vigorous campaign against the employment of women.

The state and party bureaucracy absorbed many workers as did, after 1935, the armed forces.

The schemes were spectacularly effective. Unemployment fell by 3 million in 2 years, while industrial production rose by 30%.

A Keynesian Parody

In a democratic country, the financing of this recovery - effectively by the printing of money - would have been inflationary.

Germany's recovery from depression was classically Keynesian. It was, however, only possible because the Nazis' political ambitions overrode any objections to the long term effects of the stimulus.
The state was not seen as the guardian of a liberated economic life.
Economic life was seen as a servant of the state.

The economic aim of Nazism was **mobilization for war!**

Prophetic Words, Again!

Keynes foresaw where the Nazi approach might lead........

Rescuing the United States

By the time **Franklin D. Roosevelt (1882-1945)** replaced **Herbert Hoover (1874-1964)** as President in the winter of 1932/3, the economic situation was catastrophic.

The national income was less than half what it had been four short years before. Nearly 13 million Americans - about one quarter of the labour force - were desperately seeking jobs. The machinery for sheltering and feeding the unemployed was breaking down everywhere under a growing burden. On the morning of Roosevelt's inauguration, every bank in America had locked its doors. It was now a matter of seeing whether a representative democracy could conquer economic collapse. It was a matter of staving off violence - even, some thought , - *revolution*.

– Arthur Schlesinger

Even Keynes was bemused by the size of the problem. He wrote to Lydia:

....Even I would hardly think that I could know what to do if I were President, though I expect I should when it came to it......

I RESPONDED WITH A BARRAGE OF MEASURES IN MY FIRST "HUNDRED DAYS."

Franklin D. Roosevelt

Although many of these measures would certainly now be seen as Keynesian, FDR himself did not regard them as part of a coherent "Keynesian" plan. He saw them as ways of relieving distress until more normal times returned.

A hotch-potch of recovery measures

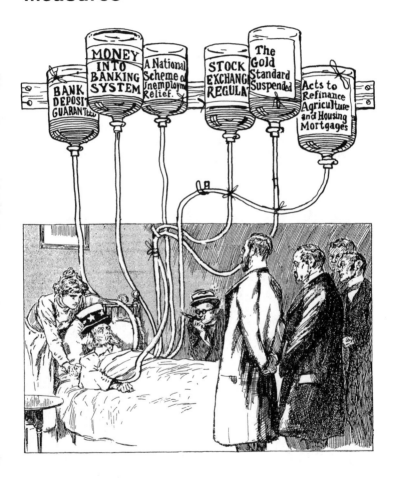

America's first experiment in state socialism was tried in the form of the Tennessee Valley Authority. There were organized, if slightly contradictory, efforts to raise both prices and wages.

On fiscal policy, Roosevelt showed his adherence to the classical balanced budget concepts by offsetting a $3.3 billion public works programme with other economies elsewhere in public spending.

And it seemed to work. There was an immediate revival in confidence. Industrial production almost doubled between March and July 1933. Keynes was sceptical as to whether the recovery would last.

ONE FEARS THE PRESIDENT IS DEPENDING FAR TOO MUCH ON PSYCHOLOGICAL AS DISTINCT FROM REAL FACTORS. THE OPERATION OF THE PSYCHOLOGICAL FACTORS IS BEING FLATTERED BY THE FACT THAT IT BEGAN AT A POINT WHEN THE USA WAS ENTITLED TO A STRONG UPWARD REACTION, EVEN WITHOUT ADVENTITIOUS AIDS. ON THE OTHER HAND, REAL FACTORS, SUCH AS OPEN-MARKET OPERATIONS AND PUBLIC WORKS ARE BEING TACKLED MUCH TOO TIMIDLY.

THUS IT IS NOT IMPOSSIBLE THAT THE PROGRAMME MAY CARRY THROUGH SUCCESSFULLY.

Keynes was hopeful that the **Multiplier** effect would be strong.

War is one solution. . . .

Whatever else it did, the **Second World War (1939-45)** solved the unemployment problem in all industrial countries. It also brought a massive increase in output.

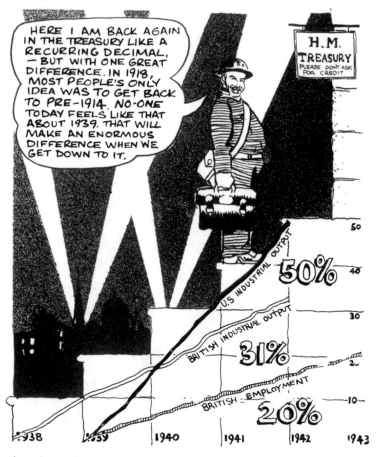

It made people determined that full employment, by whatever means, should be preserved once the war was over.

From the Cradle to the Grave

This mood was reinforced by the publication of the Beveridge Report in 1942 **(Sir William Beveridge, 1879 - 1963)**, describing itself as a plan to provide social security for all from cradle to grave. There was a general fear, rooted in the experience of the slump that followed the First World War, that mass unemployment would return again.........

UNLESS GOVERNMENTS PURSUE IT'S PREVENTION AS THEIR TOP PRIORITY

There was a general feeling throughout Europe that the Establishment of the 1930s had failed and that a fresh start must be made.

IF THE STATE CAN EFFECTIVELY MOBILIZE FOR WAR....

....IT SHOULD NOW BE ABLE TO CREATE A BETTER PEACE.

Paying for the War

Keynes' small book *How to Pay for the War* was already looking ahead. Whereas his *General Theory* had attempted to solve the problem of **deficient** demand, *How to Pay for the War* addressed the new problem of **excess** demand.

By the end of the War, Keynesian ideas were fully accepted at the Treasury. Already in 1944, the Government had published a White Paper on Employment policy....

THE GOVERNMENT ACCEPTS AS ONE OF ITS PRIMARY AIMS AND RESPONSIBILITIES THE MAINTENANCE OF A HIGH AND STABLE LEVEL OF EMPLOYMENT AFTER THE WAR.

Keynes' ideas were also accepted in the U.S. as a preventative to the horrors of the 1920s. Keynesian economics, seen essentially as a means of providing the elusive goal of full employment, had established itself as the new orthodoxy. Keynes had conquered both the academic and political worlds, not only as a solution to depressions, but for a general economic stabilization policy.

Keynesianism in War-time and After.

From the War onwards, the British Government pursued what it perceived to be Keynesian policies. The Economic section of the War Cabinet secretariat included such notable Keynesians as **James Meade** and **Richard Stone** who were extremely influencial, as was Keynes himself, over Kingsley Wood's 1941 Budget and the 1944 White Paper on employment policy.

For the remainder of the 1940s and on into the 1950s and 1960s, successive Labour and Conservative governments employed a variety of fiscal and monetary measures designed to maintain full employment without, it was hoped, causing too much inflation or damage to the balance of payments.

In the USA, Keynes' ideas were influential on government and the public's attitude to the role of government. The Employment Act of 1946 and later the Humphrey-Hawkins Act, gave the government responsibility for employment and prices.

Keynes' influence on British government policy during and immediately after the Second World War was profound. He was adroit at exploiting his personal contacts at the highest level and was personally involved in most aspects of war-time high policy both at home and in the USA.

The Bretton Woods Agreement, 27 July 1944.

The Bretton Woods conference was convened as a result of planning in both the U.S.A. and Britain by teams under Keynes in Britain and the under-secretary of the U.S. Treasury, Harry Dexter White, in the U.S. Both wanted to design a liberal economic order to avoid the harmful policies of the 1920s and 1930s when commercial warfare and competitive devaluations had brought depression and mass unemployment.

Seen here enjoying a joke at the Bretton Woods Conference, New Hampshire, last Friday are top economic experts **Harry D. White** (*left*) and **John Maynard Keynes**.

The principles behind the Bretton Woods conference were:
1. international monetary co-operation through international agencies with defined functions and powers

2. high sustained levels of international investment through the creation of of an international investment bank

3. a system of unhindered trade and convertible currencies

4. the support of gold and currency reserves to prevent short-run balance of payments deficits leading to policies with undesirable effects of unemployment

5. the balancing of payments *disequilibria* is the responsibility of both the surplus and deficit country.

International investment was to be carried out through the **International Monetary Fund** which was designed:

1. to promote international monetary co-operation through a permanent institution,

2. to facilitate the expansion of world trade and to maintain high levels of employment,

3. to promote exchange stability and to give confidence to members by making the Fund's resources available to them under adequate safeguards to correct maladjustments in their balance of payments.

The Fund came into operation on 27th December 1945 when it had 30 members. Initially its work was somewhat eclipsed by that of the **International Bank for Reconstruction and Development (World Bank)**, whose task in rehabilitating Europe and lending funds to the undeveloped nations seemed more pressing. Also in the 1940s and 1950s the liberal policies, so important to the IMF, were difficult in a world governed by exchange controls, tariffs and quotas. In 1958, the return of most European currencies to convertibility with the $ brought the IMF to the fore.

Britain's "Financial Dunkirk"

Keynes, more than anyone, appreciated Britain's precarious financial position. He warned the government that the country faced the dire prospect of a "financial Dunkirk".

Keynes was despatched by the newly elected Labour Government to negotiate a $6 billion loan from the Americans.

Furthermore, the Bretton Woods Agreement meant sterling would be freely convertible within a year and that the imperial preferences would be abandoned. Finally Britain would have to settle with her sterling creditors by 1951.

"Was the USA really ungenerous?"

The British were not the only ones clamouring for American aid. As Keynes told the House of Lords in the autumn of 1945....

"Capitalism internationally safeguarded".

Keynes pointed out that the terms negotiated were more generous than those achieved by other European countries. Furthermore they were a step along the road he had been advocating since 1920.

COFFEE?

THE OUTSTANDING CHARACTERISTIC OF THE PLANS IS THAT THEY REPRESENT THE FIRST ELABORATE AND COMPREHENSIVE ATTEMPT TO COMBINE THE ADVANTAGES OF FREEDOM OF COMMERCE WITH SAFEGUARDS AGAINST THE DISASTROUS CONSEQUENCES OF A *LAISSEZ-FAIRE* SYSTEM WHICH PAYS NO DIRECT REGARD TO THE PRESERVATION OF EQUILIBRIUM AND MERELY RELIES THE EVENTUAL WORKING OUT OF BLIND FORCES.

There was a reluctance to accept the terms. The Economist said...

OUR PRESENT NEEDS ARE THE DIRECT CONSEQUENCES OF THE FACT THAT WE FOUGHT LONGEST AND THAT WE HAVE FOUGHT HARDEST.

IN MORAL TERMS WE ARE CREDITORS; AND FOR THAT WE SHALL PAY $140 MILLION A YEAR FOR THE REST OF THE 20TH CENTURY. IT MAY BE UNAVOIDABLE BUT IT IS NOT RIGHT.

WE THREW GOOD HOUSEKEEPING TO THE WINDS. BUT WE SAVED OURSELVES AND WE HELPED TO SAVE THE WORLD!

"We've never had it so good".

Did Keynesianism work? It seemed to. For at least 25 years after the war the advanced capitalist world boomed as never before. Unemployment was lower than at any time in the previous 100 years.

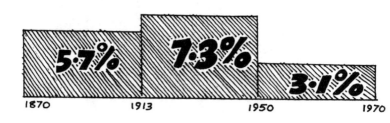

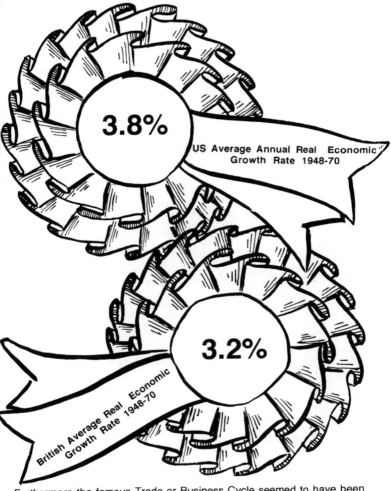

3.8%

US Average Annual Real Economic
Growth Rate 1948-70

3.2%

British Average Real Economic
Growth Rate 1948-70

Furthermore the famous Trade or Business Cycle seemed to have been tamed by Keynesian demand management. There were ups and downs in activity and levels of unemployment, but these were mild and even the downturns seemed no more than "growth recessions" constituting no more than a slowdown in the rate of growth. In 1969 Martin Brofenbrenner published a well-researched document called *"Is the Business Cycle Obsolete?"*

BOOM! No. 1

There have been arguments over how actively Keynesian governments were responsible for this boom, and other factors were put forward to explain it.

THE LONG POLITICAL SOLIDARITY OF THE ADVANCED CAPITALIST COUNTRIES, ALL OF WHOM FELT **THREATENED** BY EITHER COMMUNIST **RUSSIA** OR **CHINA**.

*THE BACKLOG OF **TECHNOLOGICAL INNOVATIONS** WAITING TO BE EXPLOITED...*

THE DEPRESSED ASPIRATIONS OF THE WORKERS, WHICH BROUGHT ABOVE-AVERAGE PERFORMANCE WITHOUT EXCESSIVE PAY DEMANDS...

*THE GROWING LIBERALIZATION OF **TRADE** UNDER **GATT**.*

GATT, the General Agreements on Tariffs and Trade, was established in Geneva in 1947 and became operational on 1st January 1948. It's main role has been to conduct a series of tariff negotiations working on two principles from its Articles of Agreement.

1. Trade should be conducted on the basis of non-discrimination between countries.

2. Existing preferential arrangements should be gradually reduced through negotiation until they are finally eliminated.

Although GATT was hampered by its lack of powers to compel nations to dismantle controls, over the following 40 years it was successful in gradually reducing restrictions on international trade.

The "Fine-Tuning" of Keynesianism.

Indeed, Keynes himself never advocated the "fine-tuning" tactics employed by successive British governments, but rather the strategic "socialization of investment" whereby action should be taken to encourage investment in both the public and private sectors.

Nevertheless governments pursued active Keynesian policies and recognized the need to take expansionary fiscal action when faced with the collapse of demand. In Britain Keynesian policies were pursued continuously untill the mid 1970s.

Fine-Tuning Demand.

On a number of occasions in the early and late 1950s, early 60s and early 70s, demand fell below the productive potential. The government responded with a combination of measures to increase effective demand.

Fiscal Policies.
-increases in government expenditure
-reductions in taxes

INFLATIONARY!

Monetary Policies
-reductions in interest rates
-relaxation of controls on bank advances and hire purchase.

MORE CREDIT!

Phillips Curve

In the late 1950s, A.W. Phillips studied Britain's economy for the previous 100 years and noted that there had been an inverse relationship between the level of unemployment and the rate of increase of money wages. When unemployment was high, wages increased slowly but when it was low, they increased a good deal faster. Common sense would suggest the reasons.

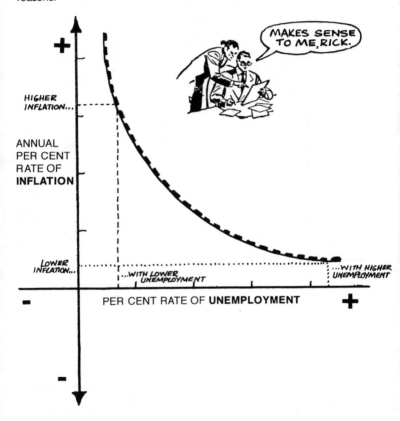

It was suggested that people would have to settle for a trade-off between levels of inflation and unemployment.

"What happens when unemployment and inflation BOTH increase?"

In the late 1960s and 70s the Phillips Curve moved up **and** to the right as both unemployment and inflation rose together.

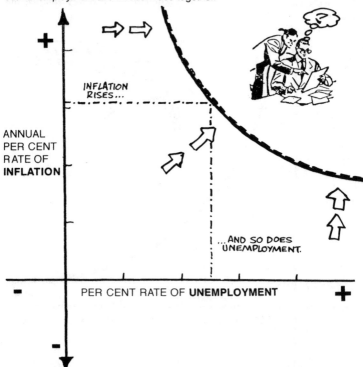

By the middle of the 1970s, people were fed up with both Keynes and Phillips, who no longer seemed able to provide a cure for either unemployment or inflation. Critics of Keynes had always pointed to the dangers inherent in budget deficits, most notably inflation, but for the 25 years after the War, inflation scarcely posed any threat. In the USA it averaged 2.5% and in Britain 4.1%. This was high by earlier standards, but not by those of the 1970s.

132

Meanwhile, in the USA.....

Jack Kennedy's administration was full of committed Keynesians determined to achieve full employment.

Eisenhower before him had been more interested in eliminating inflationary tendencies through fiscal expansion.

I'M CONCENTRATING ON THE PRE-KEYNESIAN TENDENCY OF TRYING TO BALANCE THE FEDERAL BUDGET.

RESULT? UNEMPLOYMENT ROSE IN THE 50s AND REACHED 7% BY 1960!

Increased federal expenditure followed by tax cuts brought an 8-year boom. At the end of the 1960s the newly appointed President Nixon said.......

WE ARE ALL KEYNESIANS NOW!

Rejection of Keynes in the 1970s

The collapse of the Bretton Woods system in the early 1970s and the explosive rise in the price of commodities, especially oil, brought to an end the steady, low-inflation growth the industrialized world had enjoyed since 1945.

Keynesian policies did not seem to work any more and a new *ism* came into fashion - **Monetarism**.

What is Monetarism?

The monetarist rejected the post- war Keynesian orthodoxy.

Governments should **NOT** interfere to manipulate the level of demand.

A little inflation is **NOT** acceptable to maintain full employment.

The "New" Classical Economists

The monetarists, led by their main publicist, Milton Friedman (b.1912), seemed to be going back to the 19th century classical economists of whom Keynes had been so critical.

A MODERN ECONOMY IS SELF-STABILIZING AT FULL EMPLOYMENT.

"MARKETS CLEAR" — MEANING ALL PRICES, INCLUDING LABOUR, ADJUST IN SUCH A WAY AS TO EQUATE SUPPLY AND DEMAND.

THERE IS NO INVOLUNTARY UNEMPLOYMENT.

The Natural Rate of Unemployment

Monetarists criticized attempts by Keynes-inspired goverments to keep unemployment at below the so-called "natural rate".

If this inflation rate was regarded as too high because of past mistakes then the money supply would have to be reduced in order to lower the rate of inflation, even if, in the short term, this meant *higher* unemployment.

"And what about HIGH unemployment?"

If this left unemployment high, the answer was not to try and reduce unemployment below its natural rate, but to reduce the natural rate itself. This would have to be done not by macro-economic measures but by micro-economic or what became known as "supplyside" measures.

In the monetarists view, trade unions had grown too powerful and inflexible. (Keynes wasn't a great fan of unions either.) In the 60s and 70s, union inflexibility was held to blame for

unemployment and inflation rising together.

141

The "Selsdon Man" Monetarist

Prime Minister Edward Heath (for a time nicknamed "Selsdon Man", following a Tory front-bench conference at the Selsdon Park Hotel from which tough "monetarist" pronouncements emerged), began to flirt with monetarist policies from 1970. He shrank back as unemployment breached the **1 million** mark in early 1972.

Even the Labour government of the late 1970s was forced to adopt what some considered to be anti-Keynesian policies following the financial crisis of 1976. Prime Minister Callaghan told the disbelieving delegates at the 1976 Labour Party Conference.....

Now, for Selsdon Woman!

It was Prime Minister Margaret Thatcher who embraced the monetarist policy of reducing the money supply and trying to improve the supply-side of the economy.

The main target of the monetarists and Mrs Thatcher were the unions, who, she said, had long been abusing their monopoly power to keep wages above the market clearing rate.

The closed-shop union strategy had prevented those who were prepared to work for the "market" rate from doing so.

If real wages fell, more would be employed. A fall in the natural rate of unemployment was the monetarists' main aim.

Monetarist Remedies for Unemployment

The stance of monetary policy should be judged by the behaviour of the money supply rather than that of interest rates. Inflation, leading to unemployment, is caused by an excess of money. Therefore, to reduce inflation and ultimately unemployment, the supply of money must be cut back.

Monetary policy is the **control of credit** both in terms of supply and interest rates, whereas fiscal policy is essentially **taxation**. Monetary policy, rather than fiscal policy, should be used as the more powerful instrument of stabilization policy.

The time-lags of policy measures are long and unsure in their effects on natural fluctuations in the private sector. Governments would do better to refrain from attempts at stabilization and concentrate on preventing monetary policy from becoming a destabilizing factor by fixing a target rate of growth of the money stock, irrespective of the state of effective demand.

Monetary policy can destabilize if the money supply is either too excessive or too restrictive, or if interest rates are too high or too low. If the state of effective demand is already high, releasing more money into the system or reducing interest rates (or both, as Chancellor of the Exchequer Nigel Lawson did in 1988) can lead to excess demand and increased inflation.

Friedman's views sparked off a strong academic debate and were taken up by the political right as a means of attacking state expenditure and intervention with its consequent effects of stoking up inflation.
The monetarists' timing was propitious.

Stagflation.

Milton Friedman had been working hard for almost a generation to establish the intellectual justification for his monetarist views. The stagflation (no growth combined with high inflation) of the 1970s provided the perfect backdrop for practical politicians to adopt his views, so eloquently propounded in his *Free to Choose*.

Did Monetarism Work?

In Britain, Keynesian demand management was completely abandoned. The budget deficit was reduced and the growth of money supply was slowed down.

What about the "side effects" of monetarist policy?

Milton Friedman, in support of Thatcher, said to the House of Commons Treasury and Civil Service Comittee in June 1980...

The Failure of Monetarism

Inflation did fall, though some would argue it had nothing to do with the money supply and everything to do with rising unemployment.

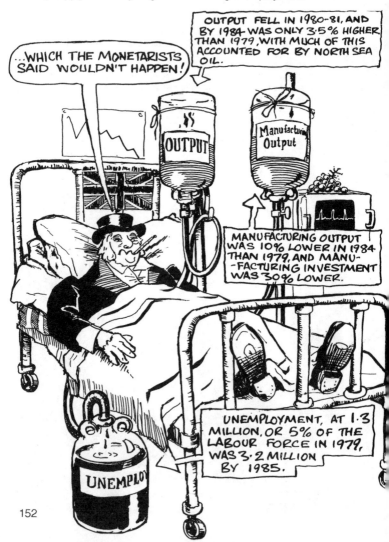

And Reaganomics?

Were things better in the USA, where President Reagan also said he was pursuing monetarist policies?
Yes.

So monetarism worked in the U.S.A.?

No.

Because whatever Reagan said or thought he was doing, he was in fact pursuing not monetarist, but **Keynesian**, policies.

The budget deficit rose from 60 billion, or 2% of Gross Domestic Product in 1980, to 200 billion or 5% of G.D.P. in 1985.

Was it fair to blame Keynesian policies for the stagflation of the 1970s?

One of the main causes of the world-wide inflation of the 1970s was the Vietnam War and the refusal of the U.S. Government to pay for it by raising taxes. Keynes would certainly have argued for raising taxes. His pamphlet, *How to Pay for the War*, had shown how increased government expenditure in war-time was inflationary.

President Johnson ignored his Keynesian advisers until 1968, by which time the "inflation horse was out of the barn".

The Contradictions of Keynes.

It could be argued that Keynesianism was blamed for a phenomenon that would never have happened, were he still alive to control events.

In analyzing Keynes, it is difficult to tie him down as he contradicted himself on certain key issues. For example, at one moment he was a strong advocate of Free Trade, saying that to argue that trade barriers reduce unemployment...

...INVOLVES THE PROTECTIONIST FALLACY IN ITS GROSSEST AND CRUDEST FORM... I BELIEVE IN FREE TRADE BECAUSE... IT IS THE ONLY POLICY WHICH IS TECHNICALLY SOUND AND INTELLECTUALLY RIGHT.

Later he spoke in favour of protection.

I SYMPATHIZE WITH THOSE WHO WOULD MINIMIZE RATHER THAN MAXIMIZE ECONOMIC ENTANGLEMENTS BETWEEN NATIONS — IDEAS, ART, HOSPITALITY, TRAVEL — THESE ARE THINGS WHICH OF THEIR NATURE SHOULD BE INTER-NATIONAL. BUT LET GOODS BE HOMESPUN WHENEVER IT IS REASONABLE OR CONVENIENTLY POSSIBLE.

Was he for the working-class or contemptuous? On the General Strike he said ..

THE STRIKERS ARE NOT REAL REVOLUTIONARIES; THEY ARE NOT SEEKING TO OVERTURN PARLIAMENT... MY FEELINGS ARE WITH THE WORKERS.

On the other hand he wrote...

Nor was he keen on trade unions.

ONCE THE OPPRESSED, NOW THE TYRANTS, WHOSE SELFISH AND SECTIONAL PRETENSIONS NEED TO BE BRAVELY OPPOSED.

He was not a great respecter of businessmen, feeling they were lazy and stupid. He saw a three-generation cycle.

He felt that Britain in the 1920s and 1930s was full of third-generation businessmen. He was to say in 1945...

IF BY SOME SAD GEOGRAPHICAL SLIP THE AMERICAN AIR FORCE (IT IS TOO LATE NOW TO HOPE FOR MUCH FROM THE ENEMY) WERE TO DESTROY EVERY FACTORY ON THE NORTH EAST COAST AND IN LANCASHIRE (AT AN HOUR WHEN DIRECTORS WERE SITTING THERE AND NO ONE ELSE), WE SHOULD HAVE NOTHING TO FEAR.

HOW ELSE WE ARE TO REGAIN THE EXUBERANT INEXPERIENCE WHICH IS NECESSARY, IT SEEMS, FOR SUCCESS, I CANNOT SURMISE.

On the other hand, he was very friendly with the businessman **Samuel Courtauld (1876-1947)**. Keynes appreciated the need to encourage business investment to bring growth and reduce unemployment.

And businesses must have the expectation of profit.

"Such expectations partly depend on non-monetary influence, on peace and war, inventions, laws, race, education, population and so forth. But their power to put their projects into execution on terms which they deem attractive almost entirely depends on the behaviour of the banking and monetary system".

Myths about Keynes

There are also myths that have grown up about Keynes.
The first is that he was tolerant of inflation.
This was not so.
He opposed it throughout his life.

The second is that he was an advocate of what became known as "fine-tuning", i.e. short-term tinkering with fiscal policy to try and iron out fluctuations in the business cycle. British governments since the war have constantly indulged in such fine-tuning. One of the favourites, especially in the 1960s and 1970s, was the change of credit restrictions on the purchase of consumer durables. Keynes was not in favour of such short-term activities.

Keynes, the Gold Standard and the ERM

There is an interesting and important Keynesian lesson to be drawn from comparing the Gold Standard of the 1920s and 30s with the attempt in the late 80s to create a stable **Exchange Rate Mechanism** for European currencies.

Both the Gold Standard and the ERM were attempts to impose a stable currency discipline on the economy by ensuring that international competition would force manufacturers to keep their costs down - in both cases by **shedding labour**. Given time - unfortunately a long time, many years, even decades - the strategy might have worked and we might have finished up with low-cost, efficient industry. In modern democracies, people will not tolerate the sacrifices involved.

I KNEW THAT IN THE 1920s... ...THAT'S WHY I OPPOSED THE GOLD STANDARD...

...AND WE FORCED A DEVALUATION OF THE POUND ON BLACK WEDNESDAY FOR MUCH THE SAME REASONS!

What was behind the City speculators' rush against the pound on Black Wednesday, 16th September 1992? The exchange rate of the Pound, like other major currencies, was pegged to the strong German Deutschmark backed by high interest rates. When the US cut its interest rates in an attempt to end recession, the Dollar inevitably went into sharp fall, putting strain on all the major European currencies in the ERM. Interest rates were also high in the U.K. (15% in 1989) and recession threatened to deepen into a slump.

Prime Minister John Major was under the illusion that the British people were prepared to endure many years of deep recession to secure a magical goal of **zero inflation**. He believed this might be achieved if the Pound remained tied to an overvalued rate against the Deutschmark.

The Pound fell steeply, it came off the ERM and interest rates were immediately slashed.

The globalisation and dotcom boom

After the recession (relatively mild compared with the 1930s and 2008–9) of the early 1990s which followed the inflationary excesses of the 1980s, not only the UK but also the rest of the developed world enjoyed a long period of growth from 1993 until 2008. This was due to a number of factors.

The first was scientific development. Personal computers came into their own to the point where almost every educated person, including children, owned one. The internet became the favoured, in some cases the only, means of acquiring and disseminating knowledge and information. This led to the explosive growth in and manufacture of products connected with the internet. Secondly, telecommunications also made great technical advances and, as with computers, every man, woman and child seemed to possess a mobile (cell) phone.

To fuel the growth of these new gadgets, the world's financial system lent potential borrowers ever more money at historically low interest rates. Inflation fell from its high levels in the 1970s and 1980s helped by the production of many of these new electrical appliances and gadgets in low-cost countries such as India and China.

Who needed Keynes now? The free market, without any help from the state, was providing the good life. No one needed handouts from governments to acquire money to buy all these new gizmos. Full employment and easy credit from banks would give everyone all they needed.

So what could go wrong? That old human failing, greed, is what could and did go wrong. By the turn of the century banks throughout the world, but most notably in the USA and the UK, were lending money to people who were going to struggle to pay the interest, let alone repay the loan. Furthermore, with all this easy money sloshing around, that old monster inflation began to raise its ugly head again. In 2007 and the first half of 2008 the price of commodities – whether hard, such as copper and steel, or soft, such as food, and most notably oil – rose sharply (oil reached $147 a barrel in July 2008, whereas it had been only $20 a barrel at the turn of the century).

In the middle of 2007 the cracks began to appear and the British government was forced into nationalising a bank, Northern Rock. During 2008 the US government first organized the rescue of a major bank, Bear Stearns, and then let one collapse (Lehman Brothers). This set off a worldwide crisis, which by early 2009 had led to predictions of a depression of 1930s proportions.

How would Keynes have reacted?

First, he would not have stood idly by as the lending boom gathered pace. He would have been alarmed by the growth of financial deregulation. He could be very scathing about banks. He said in the 1930s:

When the capital development of a country becomes a by-product of the activities of a casino, the job is likely to be ill-done.

Will Hutton wrote in the *Observer* in late 2008 about what he thought Keynes would have done:

> For Keynes, the interaction of the financial system with the real economy is capitalism's existential problem. Banks are where our savings reside without any promissory note about when we intend to spend them, so that the spectre permanently hovers over the economy of there either being too little spending or too much. The job of finance is to recycle those savings back into investment and so sustain overall levels of demand, production and employment at a balanced rate.

Friedrich Hayek, who profoundly disagreed with Keynes and who was lauded by Margaret Thatcher and her supporters, nevertheless said that Keynes was

> the one really great man I ever knew, and for whom I had unbounded admiration.

Come back, Keynes. We need you.

Keynes is back!

Publications of John Maynard Keynes

Indian Currency and Finance

Economic Consequences of the Peace

A Tract on Monetary Reform

A Treatise on Money - The Pure Theory of Money

A Treatise on Money - The Applied Theory of Money

The General Theory of Employment, Interest and Money

A Treatise on Probability

Bibliography

Keynes, Beveridge and Beyond **Tony Cutter, Karen Williams and John Williams** (Routledge and Kegan Paul, 1986)

The Making of Keynes' General Theory **Richard F. Kahn** (Cambridge University Press, 1984)

J. M. Keynes in Retrospect **Ed. Derek Crabtree and A. P. Thirlwall** (Macmillan, 1980)

Macroeconomics after Thatcher and Reagan **John N. Smithin** (Edward Egar, 1990)

The Cambridge Apostles; The Early Years **Peter Allen** (Cambridge University Press, 1978)

The Life of John Maynard Keynes **R.F. Harrod** (Macmillan, 1951)

Maynard Keynes - An Economist's Biography **D.E. Moggridge** (Routledge,1992)

Keynes' Monetary Thought **D Patinkin** (Duke University Press, 1976)

Bloomsbury Portraits **Richard Shone** (Phaidon, 1976)

John Maynard Keynes Vol.1, Hopes Betrayed 1883–1920 **Robert Skidelsky** (Viking, 1985)

John Maynard Keynes Vol.2, The Economist as Saviour 1921–37 **Robert Skidelsky** (Macmillan, 1992)

Never Again, Britain 1945–51 **Peter Hennessey** (Jonathan Cape, 1992)

The People's Peace, British History 1945–1989 **Kenneth O. Morgan** (Oxford University Press, 1990)

One of Us **Hugo Young** (Macmillan, 1989)

Post-War Britain **Alan Sked and Chris Cook** (Penguin, 1979)

The State We're In **Will Hutton** (Jonathan Cape, 1995)

John Maynard Keynes ed. **Soumitra Sharma** (Edward Elgar, 1998)

The Keynesian Revolution **Essays of Robert Eisner** (Edward Elgar, 1998)

Keynesianism and the Keynesian Revolution in America ed. **O.F. Hamouda** and **B.B. Price** (Edward Elgar, 1998)

From Boom to Bust **David Smith** (Penguin, 1992)

The Chancellors **Roy Jenkins** (Macmillan, 1998)

Margaret Thatcher, the Downing Street Years **Margaret Thatcher** (HarperCollins, 1993)

The Keynesian Revolution and its Economic Consequences **Peter Clarke** (Edward Elgar, 1998)

Acknowledgements

Artwork Assistants
Glenn Ward
Sarah Garratt

Picture Research
Helen James
Deborah Wood
Maureen Mortlock

Index